I Smell Heaven

I Smell Heaven
Poems on our pets' end of life

A collection by Susan L. Trott

MINDPRESS
MEDIA
NEW YORK

Copyright © 2021 by Eric D. Boscia

All rights reserved.

No part of this book may be reproduced or transmitted in any form or by any means, electronic or mechanical, including photocopying, recording, video, or by any information or retrieval system, without prior written permission from the publisher except for the use of brief quotations in a book review.

Published in the United States by MindPress Media, New York

ISBN 978-1-7357495-1-8

For information about quantity sales, rights, and other inquiries,
please visit ISmellHeaven.com or email ISmellHeaven@gmail.com.
Proceeds from the sales of the book benefit various animal rescue agencies.

Words and drawings by Susan L. Trott
Cover and book design by Eric D. Boscia
Photography by Shutterstock

Printed in the United States of America.

Foreword

My friend Sue.

Sue Trott was creative, brash, fierce and gutsy. A copywriter, she built some of the biggest brands in the world. But at night her real passion surfaced – Sue rescued animals who had been abused and neglected. She cooked stew for Tulip, her American Bulldog, and pushed her in a stroller when the dog was infirm. She talked "baby talk" to a very snarly pit bull. "Don't be scared," she told him. "Mommy is here to help you, Sweet Baby."

Once, to celebrate one of my achievements, Sue insisted that I wear her new expensive "wonder woman bracelet" – "because YOU FOUND YOUR POWER!" she crowed. She pulled clothes out of her closet to dress me, introduced me to Century 21 Department Store, and taught me to find Gaultier treasures buried in the discount racks. Sue championed my strengths, encouraged me in moments of weakness, and was the epitome of love for all creatures, human and other. Sue was wrested away from us but left this book as her legacy and gift - to anyone who has loved and lost a friend.

Judy Segaloff
Journalist and PR Executive

I smell heaven

My battered muzzle's flecked with gray
And my eyes no longer clear
But my deaf ears can still hear the sound
Of angels drawing near.

My dry old nose is twitching
From exciting, distant smells
It's the delights of doggy heaven
That are waiting, I can tell.

It's not into the darkness
That these once-keen senses call
But light and joy and running free
And perhaps a tennis ball.

And when, in many years,
Your own time has come,
I'll put down the stick I'm chewing
Or wake from napping in the sun.

You'll know how to find the place
Where, with wagging tail, I'll be.
Just follow your nose
And it will lead you straight to me.

Leaving quietly

So softly did you prowl the house
So delicate your play
That when it was your time to go
I didn't hear you slip away.

But last night when I was sleeping
I felt footsteps near my head
A silent little shadow
Returning to your spot upon the bed.

Then, this morning by the kitchen sink
I felt a brush of silky fur
Out from a shaft of sunlight
Came a low, contented purr.

It's a comfort knowing you can still visit home
Where your gentle life was spent
Coming back to me in spirit
As quietly as you went.

A mess in heaven

Angels, better get out the mops
The cleaning sprays and wipes
My big old boy is coming
He'll be with you tonight.

His enormous paws will leave a trail
As they did throughout my house
And more food will land on your spotless clouds
Than ends up in his mouth.

And he does like to chew his greasy bone
On freshly-laundered sheets
Then stomp and dig and rearrange
Until the bed's a wrinkled heap.

I can't promise you he won't lift his leg
On your sparkling Pearly Gates
Or when he's wet and muddy,
Won't stand next to you and shake.

But he's a gentle, affectionate boy
Who's looking for a hug from those above
He may slobber on your celestial robes
But it's not drool, it's love.

Last confession
of a naughty dog

A little dog sitting by Heaven's Gates
Ready to go in
Paused and said, "Before I do
I'd like to ask forgiveness for my sins.

Tell my mistress I regret
I ate your brand new shoes
My mistake, I thought you said
That they were Jimmy Chews.

Forgive me for the time
I got in your undie drawer
And wore a bra-hat on my head
And then there were those puddles on the floor.

Yes, it was me who dug up the bed
Looking for a bone
And there was that shredded toilet paper
You found when you got home.

God, with all your angels here
I know I could mend my naughty ways
Then my mistress will forgive me
When she arrives someday."

God replied, "Your contrition does you credit
And it's important that you try
But your mistress loves you as you are
And as your Creator, so do I.

It's in my power to make you a different dog
One who always did as he was bid
But you would no longer be her little devil
And she'd never forgive me if I did."

Blue heaven

My life was spent swimming back and forth
Just me, in this place with four glass sides
Adorned with plants and bubbling pirate's chest
And a little castle in which to hide.

Daily, tasty fish flakes would shower down
So I didn't have to search for food
Or worry I'd be a bigger fish's dinner
So in some sense, my life was good.

But soon I feel the time is coming
When my graceful fins must wave farewell
I'm truly grateful for the days we spent
And for your serving me so well.

Know my heaven will be a vast blue world
Not confined by tanks or bowls
I'll swim to far horizons as I was meant to
As I join an ocean full of souls.

One last thing

When my ball rolled underneath the couch
You'd get on your hands and knees
You patiently sift through my food
To take out those round things you call peas.

You were ready to scratch those itchy places
Behind my ears and under my chin
And in your pajamas, go out at midnight
When I couldn't hold it in.

You've given me tasty bits right off your plate
Even though you were peckish too
But now there's one more sacrifice
That I must ask of you.

Please release me from these aches and pains
And understand it's time for me to go
Because you love me so unselfishly
I know you won't have the heart to say no.

Well worn

Like your soft, much-washed blanket
Or that favorite toy you chewed
Your dear old body's tattered,
But I prefer to say, well-used.

I know each dent in your familiar coat
The nick that decorates your ear
And remember all the rambunctious fun
That put each mark here.

If you choose to shed this earthly form
That is for you to do
Know that I would never trade my used boy
For a shiny new one of you.

I will catch you

You always were a clumsy girl
A dog with four left feet.
Today, you nearly stumbled
As we walked slowly down the street.

Unlike in the past, I could not laugh
It hurts to see you getting old.
There are days I have to help you stand
On legs that will not hold.

But as I have always done,
I promise I'm right here
Should your once-strong legs fail you
I'll catch you, never fear.

And remember, when into that final sleep
At last you softly fall,
Heavenly arms will reach to help you,
The ones who will catch us all.

Safe places

We rabbits inhabit a dangerous world
And must be ready to run for our lives
From fearsome beasts with fangs and claws
And hungry humans carrying knives.

But you gave me a place that's calm and safe
Inside its walls, I could happily explore
With a handy couch to hide behind
When noisy strangers came to the door.

My kind would consider it rabbit heaven
Filled with treats and scampers down the hall
But (as they've whispered in strictest confidence)
In Our Real Heaven, that's not all.

Heaven's fields are lush, green, and rolling
But quieter and softer than a cloud
No predators to interrupt our exuberant romps
And where cruel people are not allowed.

There, we can emerge from our cozy burrows
And play without fear of being snatched
Or nibble peacefully at the endless salad bar
From the angels' special garden patch.

Maybe those gentle helpers will sometimes hold me
As a reminder that earthly life had its own charms
So I won't forget the feeling of contentment
Every time I hopped into your arms.

Pearly Gatecrasher

He was the biggest cat I ever saw
With a bottom like a pear
He almost tipped it over
When he climbed onto a chair.

You couldn't bar him from a room
When he put his weight against the door.
He once stole a whole roast turkey
And dragged it to the floor.

Now, among heaven's willowy angels
There's a new one, strong and stout
It's not so much they let him in
It's just they couldn't keep him out.

Running ahead

On daily walks, you raced ahead
Your dancing feet would fly
Through summer grass and snowfalls
And so the happy years went by.

But now time has slowed your steps
They're weak and filled with pain
Your dimming eyes are telling me
You have to go ahead again.

"Let me gently slip the leash of life
This you must help me do."
So go, dear friend, find heaven's joys
Until I can follow you.

A missing friend

He was taken to the vet
And never did come come
Suddenly, there's just one of me
And I'm feeling so alone.

In the corner is the carrier
That I saw you put him in
But now it's standing empty
And his scent is growing dim.

I've searched and searched around the house.
Looking everywhere
In all his favorite hiding places
Behind the couch, under the stairs.

Is that him walking past the mirror,
His furry shape I see?
Oh silly, I keep forgetting
That dog in there is me.

Wait, is that him standing by the door?
Bathed in a pool of golden light?
Yes, it's his soft woof calling me
His wagging tail a joyous sight.

But there's something changed about him
His old body's young and strong again
I knew he wouldn't leave his friend behind
He just left behind his pain.

Just resting

At running, jumping and catching balls
If I may say, I was the best
But now that my allotted time is done,
I think I'll take a well-earned rest.

In heaven, I'll drift off to sleep
And with a downy cloud for my bed
I'll dream of those who loved me
Before my earthly form was shed.

Soon, I'll wake refreshed, more like myself
Having made a complete recovery
Restored, the energy and strength
Those last days took out of me.

I'll be back to running and jumping joyously
So, for sadness, there is no cause.
My playfulness is not forever stilled
But only temporarily put on "paws."

A borrowed dog

I wasn't his real owner
Just minding him for a friend
When they called and said
Our visits were at an end.

My sometimes little house guest
Had fallen sick and died
He didn't have to be mine
To know the reasons why they cried.

I too had shared his happy
explorations in the park,
His tailspins when he saw you
And his joyful, whining bark.

His snoring warmth upon my bed
Cuddling while we watched TV
No, he was not my dog
But those memories belong to me.

Flying free

I was content inside my little cage
I know you gave me love
But I glimpsed the sky outside my window
With its white clouds high above.

One day soon, I'll spread my wings
As my unfettered soul takes flight
Climbing higher than the clouds
Following the light.

There to find a mighty tree
With strong branches for my roost
With whispering leaves to shade me
And heaven for my roof.

Listen then, for my joyous song
Carried on the wind
And do not mourn my life that's gone
Delight in the one I will begin.

Last licks

As dog etiquette demands, I must thank you
Though I've always tried to express it in the past
But there won't be another opportunity for a while
As my time has come at last.

I want to acknowledge your many kindnesses
For example, when I knew you had a busy day
You'd still take the time to fetch a treat
Or go outside and play.

And when nature inconveniently called me
In rain or snow or gloom of night
You'd complete the task in all weathers
Like that mailman I try not to bite.

You'd patiently wipe food spills off my front
Comb my coat free of leaves and burrs
Thanks for understanding the high maintenance
Involved when you have fur.

So I'll be sure to mention your unselfish acts
As I pass through the flap in heaven's doors
Someday, we'll have all the time we didn't get on earth
When you too, lay down the burden of life's chores.

But for now, can you bring your face a little closer?
Let me give you a grateful lick before I go
So you'll have something special to remember
Until the lick I'll give you to say hello.

Sad eyes

You'd turn those big brown eyes on me
They'd cut through my resistance like a drill
You knew it was a sure-fire trick
A gentle ploy to work your will.

Any tasty treat you craved
It was yours without a fight
It's how you coaxed just one more walk
Even when I'd packed up for the night.

How I miss that sweet expression
In eyes that closed for the final time
Until we meet again in heaven
The sad eyes will be mine.

Midnight

Humans think heaven's filled with sunshine
Where their souls can bask in golden light
True, its warmth is good for catnaps
But felines much prefer the night.

We imagine heaven is a velvet darkness
Filled with rustling, twitchy sounds
Inviting us to investigate
As we make our nightly rounds.

There cats socialize and groom each other
Eyes glowing under a silver moon
Lately I've heard their distant, yowling calls
Telling me that I'll be among them soon.

So will our heaven be dark or light?
A question that piques our natural curiosity
Still, I'm content to wait until I get there
Because cats also love a mystery.

Bargains

Pocket Pet, that's what it said
Above me, on the pet shop sign
And today, I was specially reduced!
Just $7.99!!

Not much in out-of-pocket costs
Some say because I'm not like a dog or cat
Those are real pets you can play with
Whereas I just sit there and that's that.

But you made an effort to enrich a life
That to others, was no big deal
Allowed me to explore the house
Instead of endless running in a wheel.

You googled how to supplement my diet
With special treats you thought I might enjoy
And sometimes those packages from Amazon
Contained a bouncy, jingly toy.

Sadly, we don't have the longevity your species does
I wish we could have shared a few years more
But in my short life, I knew love and adventure
And that was much more than I bargained for.

That was me

That sudden movement you thought you saw
Out of the corner of your eye
Or a rush of emotion that came from nowhere
That almost made you cry.

That sound you heard in a quiet room
That could be mistaken for a bark
A dream where I still trotted next to you
To our favorite places in the park.

That photo where my eyes seemed to speak to you
Of gratitude for all you did for me.
Feeling that flowed out to comfort you
Which logic says it couldn't be.

No, it's not a figment of your imagination
Or a way to deal with the sad reality
Simply check with your heart and not your mind
And you'll realize all of that was me.

You spent your life attending to
A dog's appointed tasks.
Watering every tree in sight
Without waiting to be asked.

You searched for all the choicest sticks,
Then mulched them, piece by piece.
Tirelessly pulled stuffing from your toys
Until your mouth was filled with fleece.

You kept a watchful eye on the front door
Protecting it from pizza delivery guys.
And in summer, helped with pest control
By chasing buzzy flies.

Soon, when you arrive at heaven's door
Where all earthly deeds must be summed,
When asked how you did in life
You can truly say job well done.

Serpent in paradise

Yessss, they let snakes into heaven.
We are God's creatures after all
We can only apologize for the part we played
In Man and Woman's fall.

But let's let bygones be bygones.
Heaven's where old hates do not exist
There I can stretch out on a rock
And sun myself in the warmth of divine bliss.

I'll meet again my earthly prey
Fellow creatures I was once compelled to eat
And make friends, not meals, of them
In their forgiveness, my joy's complete.

No longer reviled and feared by all
My inner nature will come through
At last to receive the love and acceptance
In life, I only got from you.

One of a kind

Why do people say get another dog or cat
Like it's just a replacement part
Just install a new one in your home
And instantly, you've fixed your broken heart.

It's something the well-meaning tell you
Thinking it will help you through the grief.
Not knowing each life is like a snowflake
Unique and sadly just as brief.

Not a flat tire, or burned-out light bulb
Or some old sweater with a hole
Each dog, cat, bird or bunny
Is a special being with a soul.

But yes, we do get "others"
Because, by a simple twist of fate,
Our beloved one could have been the pet
Left unchosen in a tiny crate.

Together, we can help each other heal
For they too, are feeling life's pain.
And we will experience love again
Though we will never love the same.

Retired

Like a baseball jersey number
Once belonging to a "great"
There's a small part of my grieving heart
That to you, I dedicate.

Of course, there will be others.
I can't ignore those desperate for a home.
But that special place is forever put aside
For you, and you alone.

Heaven can wait

I took my time getting from A to B
Since I had no pressing place to go
No hungry predators to flee from
Safe in the stout walls of my bowl.

Paddling in my little pool
Or climbing onto a relaxing rock
Was, by nature, a slow-motion affair
We turtles don't live by the clock.

We're also slow in our affections
To emerge from the privacy of our shell
Please don't think I was stand-offish
If I took the time to know you well.

We answer heaven's call slowly too
When our time on earth is at an end
Which will give me ample opportunity
To say thanks for being my friend.

Au revoir

The French have an expression
When loved ones have to part
That adds a ray of hope to moments
That might otherwise break your heart.

It implies that we will not say goodbye
Because the bonds between us are so strong
No matter how far you go, I'll find you
Though the intervening years are long.

Someday we'll see each other in the distance
And with heavenly wings upon our feet
And arms outstretched, race towards each other
Until at last, again we meet.

About the Author

A brilliant artist and clever writer, a native New Yorker, Susan L. Trott, created some of the most memorable advertising campaigns in the most prestigious advertising agencies in London and New York City. Her work experience spanned BBDO, J. Walter Thompson, McCann-Erickson and Saatchi & Saatchi, where she won awards for her campaigns for top international brands. Coke, Pepsi, and SONY were just a few of her name-brand clients.

She went on to form her own company, mentoring many in the creative art of advertising and marketing.

But Sue was not all work. She had a passion for animals and for rescuing pets. Her pit bull rescue organization, Earth Angels, saved dogs from drug dens in Harlem and paid to rehabilitate and house them. Her 'soul mate' was an American Bulldog named Tulip, and after Tulip passed away, she rescued another American Bulldog, named Pink. She lovingly prepared food for her dogs, and when they got sick and were too ill to walk, she shuttled them in baby carriages and wagons. After they died, she began writing poems. Her poetry encompassed all pets – dogs, cats, rabbits, even snakes.

In October 2018, Sue Trott was found slain in the bedroom of her NYC apartment. To date, a neighbor stands accused of the murder. Sue's love for animals – her legacy – lives on in this book of poetry, preserved and designed by her business partner and friend, Creative Director, Eric Boscia. This book perpetuates the souls of many adored pets, her own and those of her acquaintances. More importantly, it reflects the nurturing essence of Sue Trott, who believed a spirit never dies.

Please visit www.ismellheaven.com

Portrait photo by Andrew Golledge

www.ingramcontent.com/pod-product-compliance
Lightning Source LLC
Chambersburg PA
CBHW061120170426
43209CB00013B/1616